THE CLASSICAL GUITAR COLLECTION

48 great classical guitar solos for intermediate to advanced level players.

© 2016 by Faber Music Ltd
First published in 2016 by Faber Music Ltd
Bloomsbury House
74–77 Great Russell Street
London WC1B 3DA
Cover design by Kenosha Design
Printed in England by Caligraving Ltd
All rights reserved

ISBN10: 0-571-53879-7
EAN13: 978-0-571-53879-9

To buy Faber Music publications or to find out about the full range of titles
available please contact your local retailer or Faber Music sales enquiries:

Faber Music Limited, Burnt Mill, Elizabeth Way, Harlow, CM20 2HX England
Tel: +44 (0) 1279 82 89 82   Fax: +44 (0) 1279 82 89 83
sales@fabermusic.com   fabermusicstore.com

CONTENTS

CONTENTS

Explanation of the following signs may be useful:
L'explication des signes suivants pourrait être utile:
Die Erklärung der folgenden Zeichen mag für den Spieler von Nutzen sein:

LH legato or slur.

M.G. legato ou liaison.

Linke Hand: legato oder Bindebogen.

L.H. finger indicated should remain on the string.
Pressure should be released for a shift to another fret.

M.G. le doigt indiqué doit rester sur la corde.
La pression doit cesser au changement de case.

Die angedeuteten linken Finger sollen auf der Saite bleiben.
Bei Bundwechsel soll der Druck aufhören.

L.H. fingers must be positioned before the ensuing phrase is played.

Les doigts de la M.G. doivent être en position avant de jouer la phrase suivante.

Bevor die nächste Phrase gespielt wird, muss die Fingerstellung der linken Hand eingenommen werden.

CIII

Grand *barré*.

Grand *barré*.

Grosser Quergriff (*barré*).

III

Barré stopping 3 strings or less.

Barré sur 3 cordes au moins.

Quergriff über 3 oder weniger Saiten.

Momentary *barré*, stopping the strings indicated by the bracket.

Barré momentané, sur les cordes indiquées entre parenthèses.

Kurzer Quergriff über die durch die Klammer bezeichneten Saiten.

Natural harmonics are shown by a diamond note-head at their true pitch, with fret and string numbers indicated. For artificial harmonics, the diamond note-head shows the note to be stopped, while the forefinger of the RH touches the string above the fret indicated.

Les harmoniques naturelles sont indiquées à la hauteur réelle par une tête de note carrée. Pour les harmoniques artificielles, la tête de note carrée indique la note à jouer, tandis que l'index droit se pose sur la corde au-dessus de la case indiquée.

Natürliche Flageolettöne weden mit viereckigen Notenköpfen in der richtigen Tonhöhe angezeigt, mit vorgeschriebenem Bund und Saitennummern. Für künstliche Flageolettöne zeigt der viereckige Notenkopf den zu stoppenden Ton, wahrend der rechte Vorderfinger die Saite über dem bezeichneten Bund berührt.

Notes indicated by the bracket to be plucked simultaneously by the RH thumb.

Les notes pourvues de parethèses sont à pincer simultanément avec le pouce droit.

Noten, die mit Klammern versehen sind, sollen gleichzeitig mit dem rechten Daumen gespielt werden.

Valtz

Op. 7 No. 6

Dionisio Aguado

Spanish Romance

Anon.

Allegretto

Asturias (Leyenda)

Isaac Albéniz

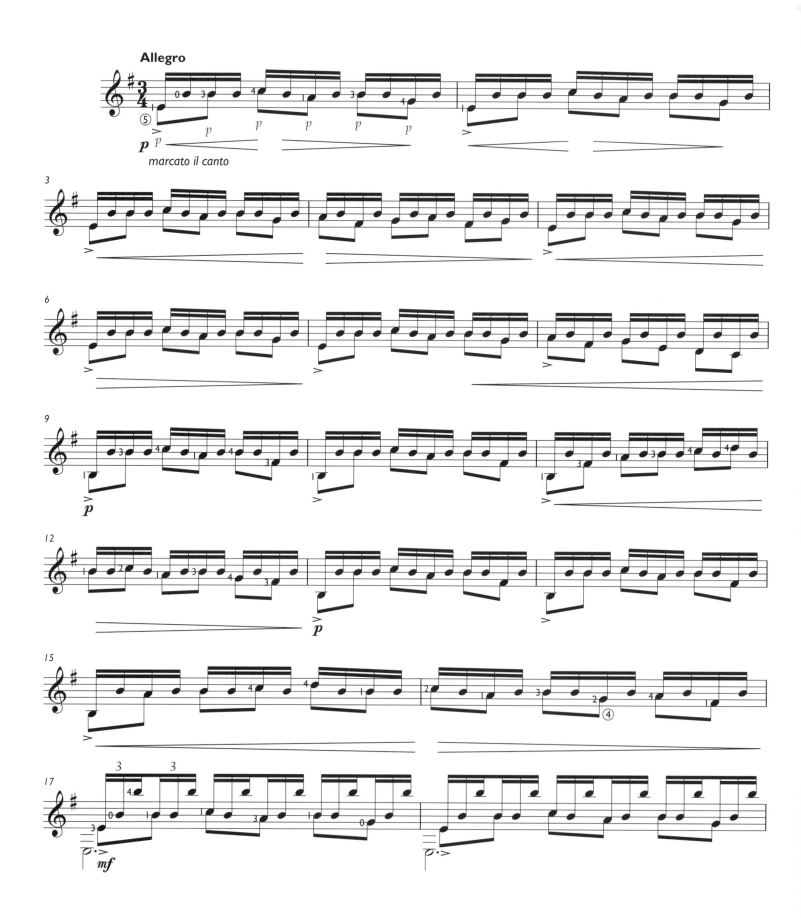

Scherzo

Malcolm Arnold

Arietta

Malcolm Arnold

I (from 'Two Preludes')

Johann Sebastian Bach

Transcribed by Julian Bream

Tune guitar:
⑥ to D

Courante (from 'Suite in E minor')

BWV 996

Johann Sebastian Bach

Transcribed by Julian Bream

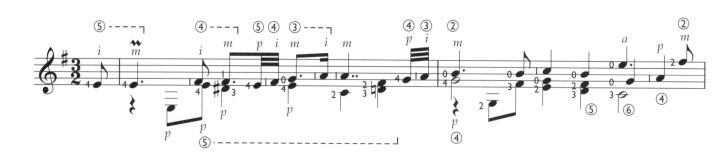

Sarabande (from 'Suite in E minor')

BWV 996

Johann Sebastian Bach

Transcribed by Julian Bream

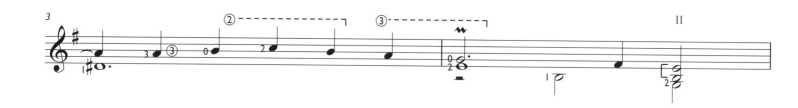

Bourrée (from 'Suite in E minor')

BWV 996

Johann Sebastian Bach

Transcribed by Julian Bream

Aria

Giuseppe Antonio Brescianello

Gavotta

Giuseppe Antonio Brescianello

Sicilienne

Op. 34 No. 2

Ferdinando Carulli

Allemande (from 'Suite in E minor')

Dieterich Buxtehude

Transcribed by Julian Bream

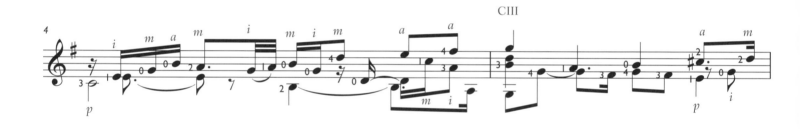

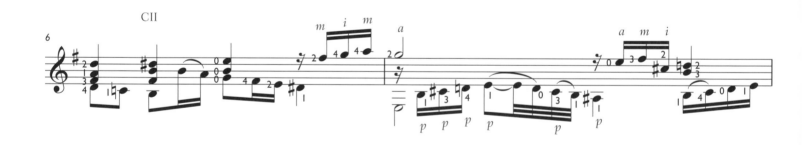

Courante (from 'Suite in E minor')

Dieterich Buxtehude

Transcribed by Julian Bream

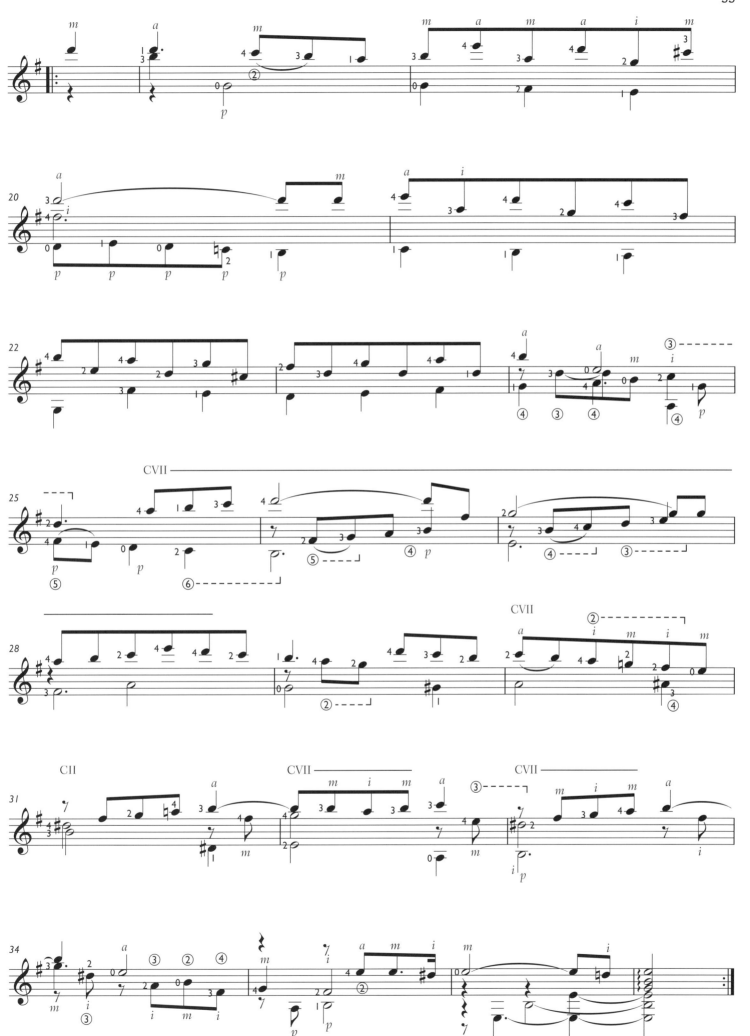

Sarabande (from 'Suite in E minor')

Dieterich Buxtehude

Transcribed by Julian Bream

Gigue (from 'Suite in E minor')

Dieterich Buxtehude

Transcribed by Julian Bream

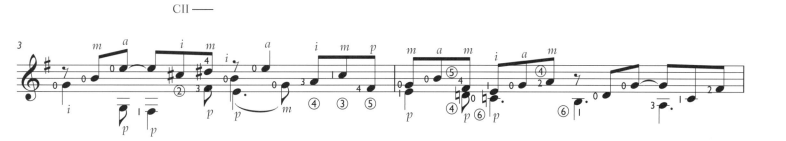

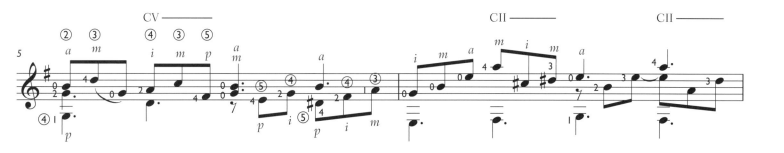

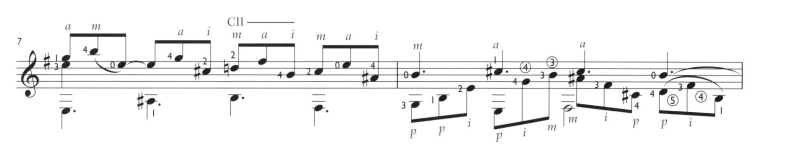

Sonata 2

Domenico Cimarosa

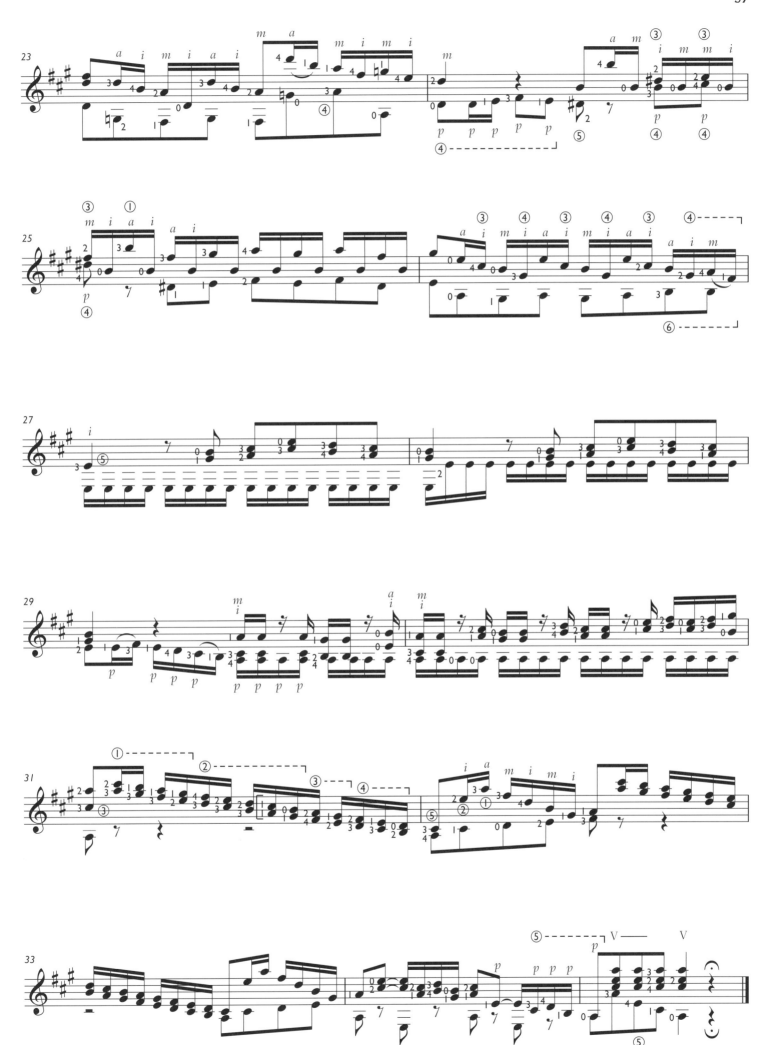

La Fille aux Cheveux de lin (from 'Two Preludes')

Claude Debussy

Transcribed by Julian Bream

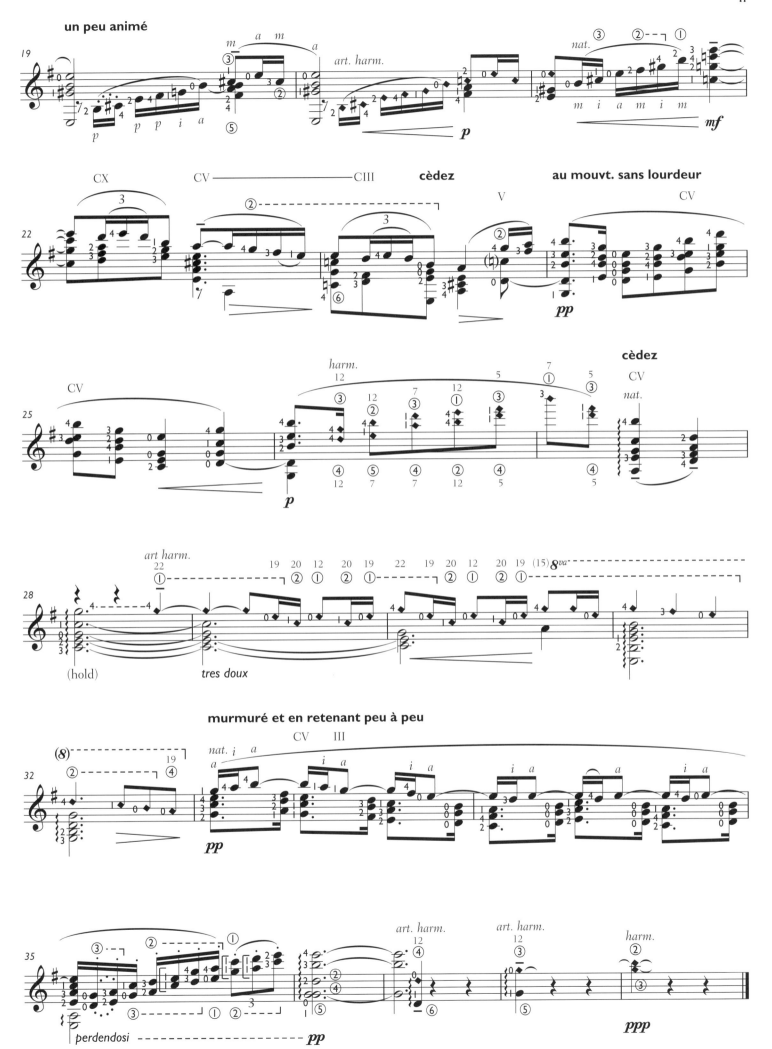

Minstrels (from 'Two Preludes')

Claude Debussy

Transcribed by Julian Bream

Modére: nerveux et avec humeur

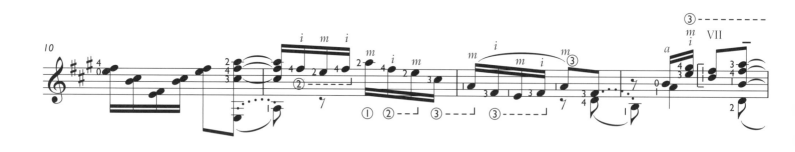

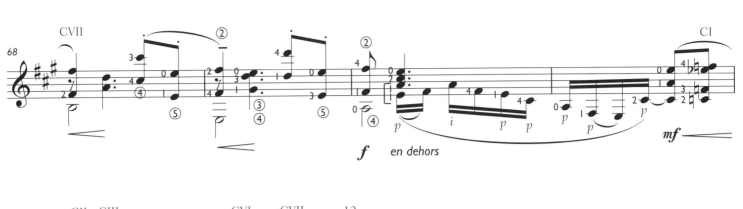

Andante Sostenuto (from 'Sonata in F major')

Anton Diabelli

Transcribed by Julian Bream

Ejercicio: Allegretto

José Ferrer

Vals

José Ferrer

Valse (from 'Lyric Pieces')

Op. 12

Edvard Grieg

Transcribed by Julian Bream

Watchman's Song (from 'Lyric Pieces')

Op. 12

Edvard Grieg

Transcribed by Julian Bream

Molto andante e semplice

Intermezzo (Ghosts at Night)

Fairy Dance (from 'Lyric Pieces')

Op. 12

Edvard Grieg

Transcribed by Julian Bream

Étude Allegro Spiritoso

Mauro Giuliani

Leçon

Mauro Giuliani

Sarabande (from 'Suite in A minor')

Johann Jacob Froberger

Transcribed by Julian Bream

Gigue (from 'Suite in A minor')

Johann Jacob Froberger

Transcribed by Julian Bream

La Catedral

Agustín Barrios Mangoré

Preludio "Saudade"

Andante religioso

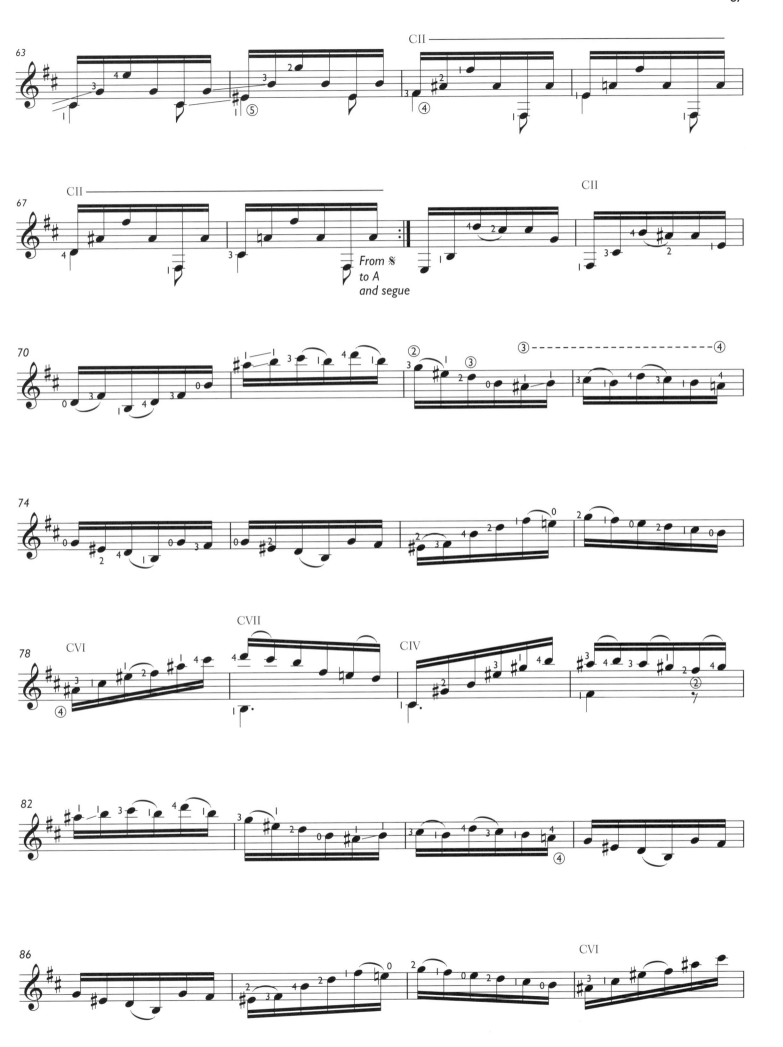

Landler
Op. 9 No. 5

Johann Kaspar Mertz

Landler

Op. 9 No. 4

Johann Kaspar Mertz

A Winter Landscape (from 'Little Suite for Guitar')

Nicholas Maw

Senza misura

Tempo I

Poco meno mosso

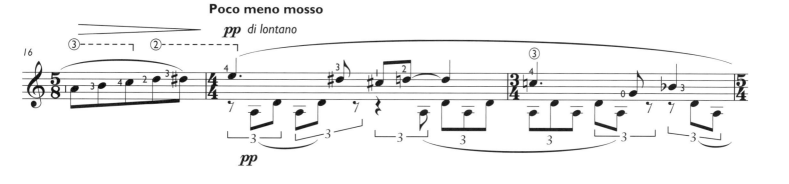

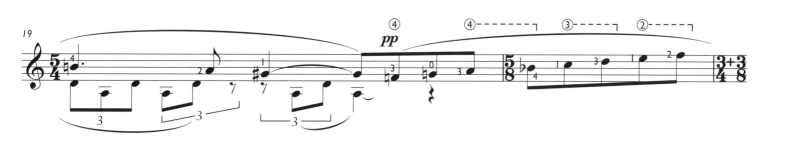

morendo

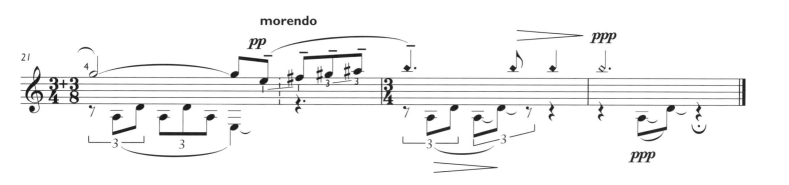

Larghetto and Allegro (from the 'Divertimento K229')

Wolfgang Amadeus Mozart

Transcribed by Julian Bream

Tune guitar:
⑥ to D

Gaillarde

Guillaume Morlaye

Air (from 'Four Pieces')

Henry Purcell

Transcribed by Julian Bream

Rondo (from 'Four Pieces')

Henry Purcell

Transcribed by Julian Bream

Minuet (from 'Four Pieces')

Henry Purcell

Transcribed by Julian Bream

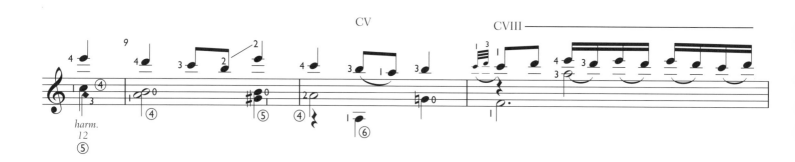

Hornpipe (from 'Four Pieces')

Henry Purcell

Transcribed by Julian Bream

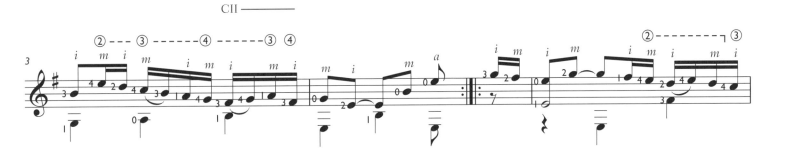

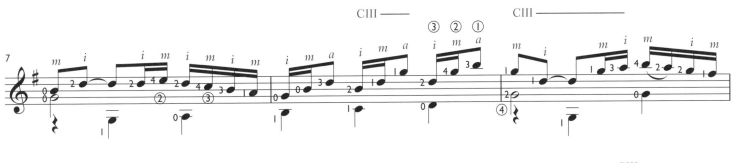

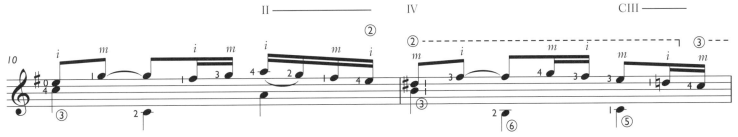

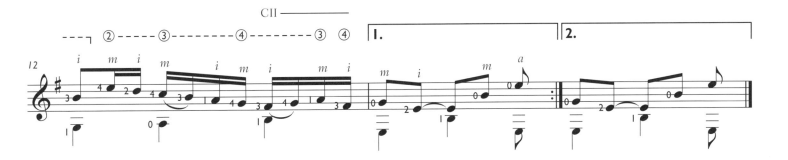

Maria Luisa: Mazurka

Julio Salvador Sagreras

Nostalgia: Petite Mélodie

Julio Salvador Sagreras

Theme with Variations

Robert Schumann

Transcribed by Julian Bream

Into The Dreaming

Peter Sculthorpe

Tuning:

⑤ to G
⑥ to D

Waltz

Op. 7 No. 1

Johann Strauss

Waltz
Op. 7 No. 3

Johann Strauss

Capricho Árabe

Francisco Tárrega

Tune guitar:

⑥ to D

poco cresc.

accel.

Recuerdos de la Alhambra

Francisco Tárrega

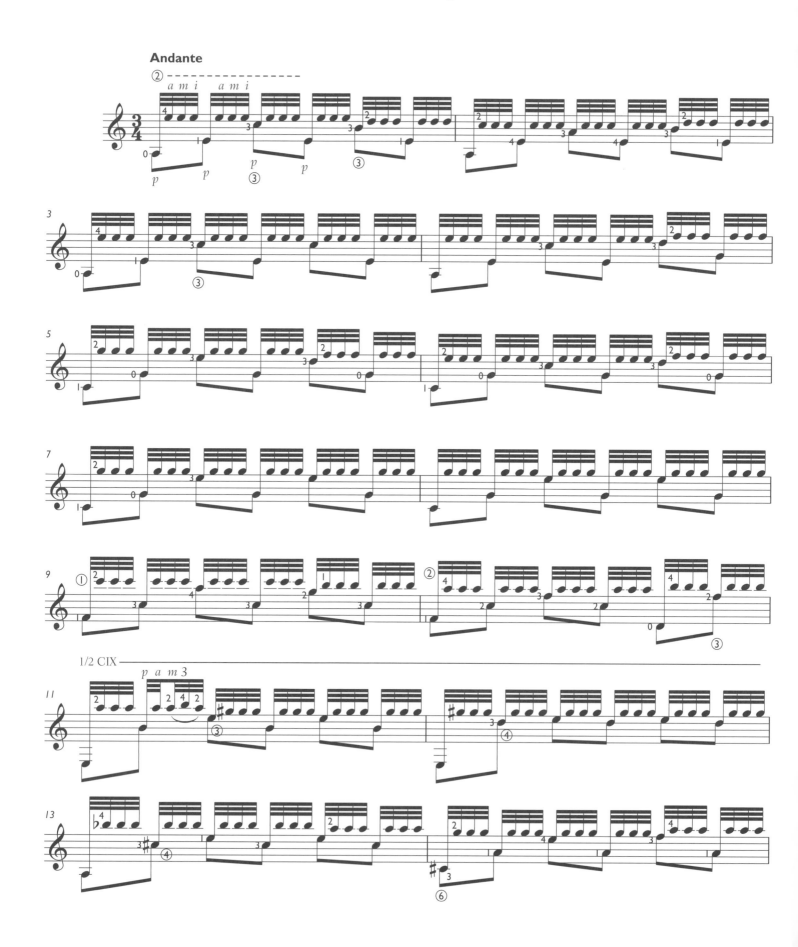

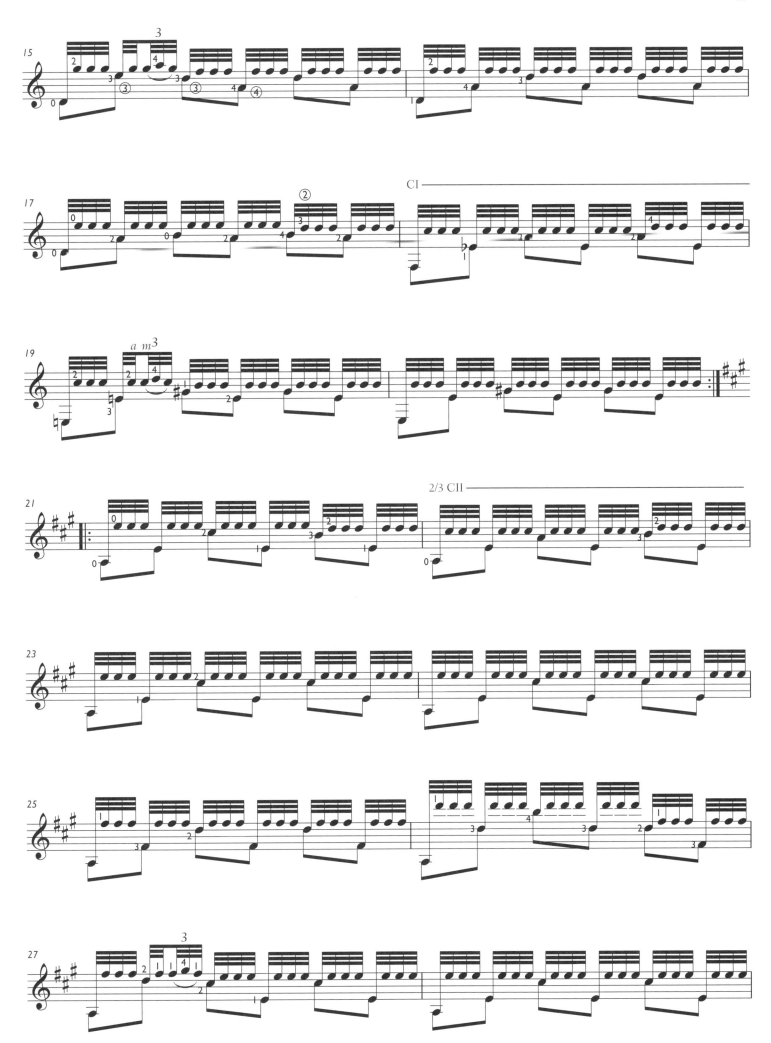

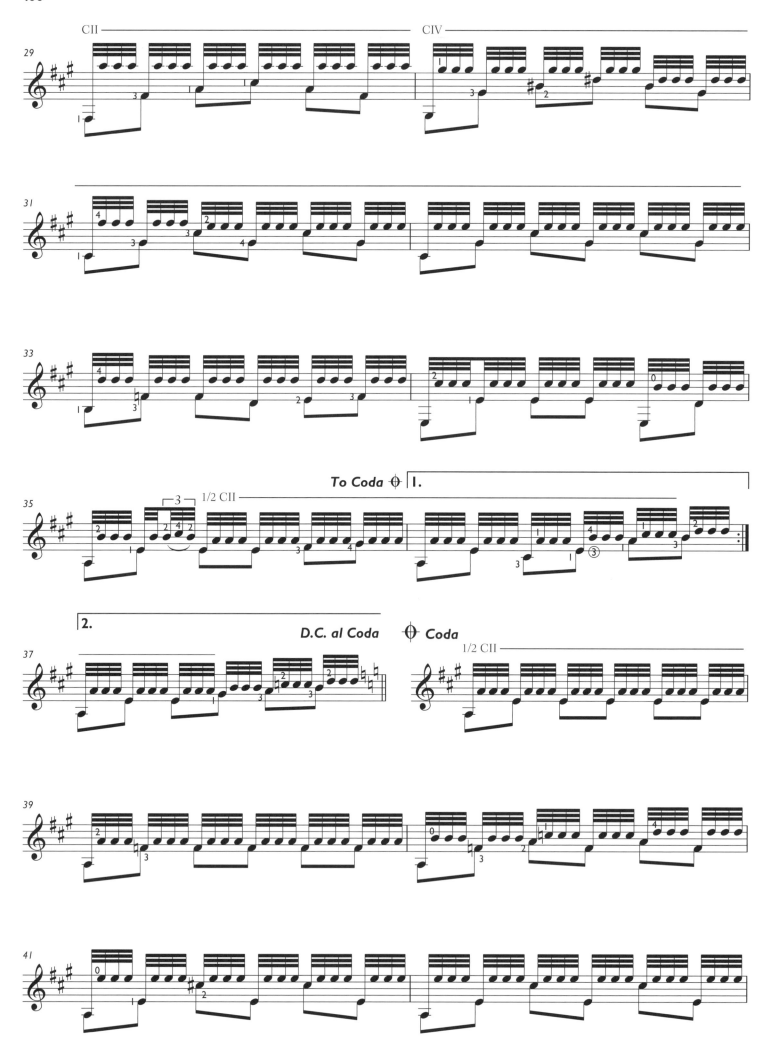

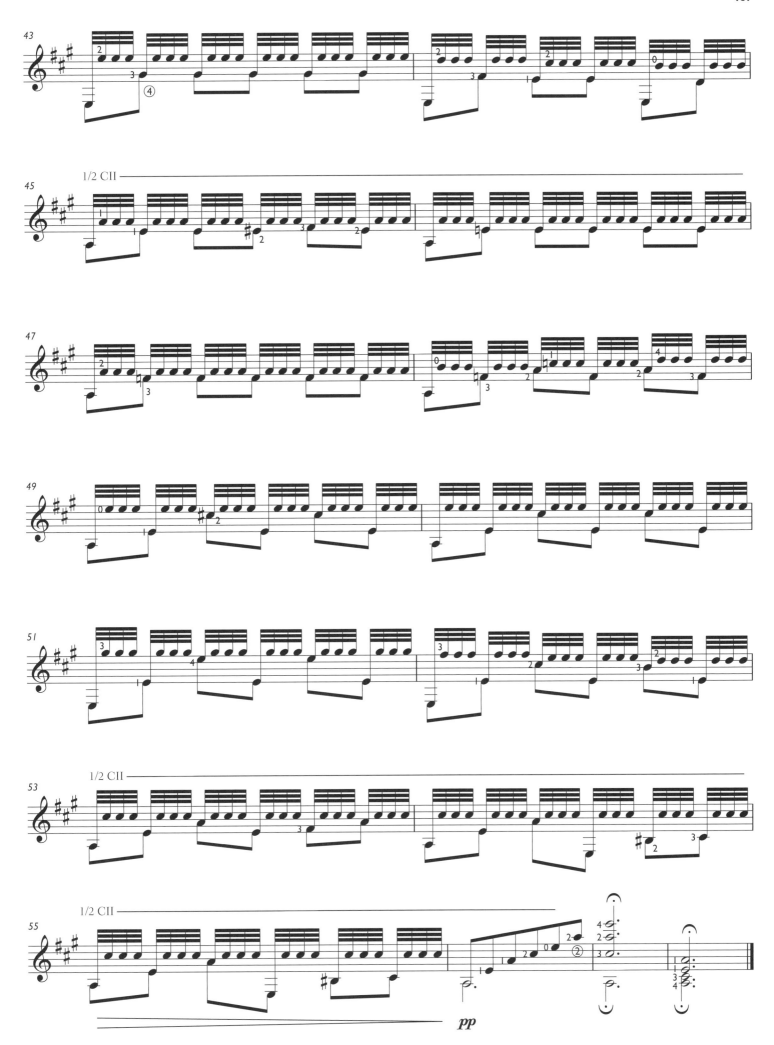

Étude

Op. 31 No. 23

Fernando Sor

Mouvement de prière religieuse